CRICKET

CLIVE GIFFORD

WAYLAND

Published in paperback in 2014 by Wayland

Copyright © Wayland 2014

Wayland
Hachette Children's Books
338 Euston Road
London NW1 3BH

Wayland Australia
Level 17/207 Kent Street
Sydney, NSW 2000

Managing Editor: Rasha Elsaeed
Produced by Tall Tree Ltd
Editor: Jon Richards
Designer: Ben Ruocco
Photographer: Michael Wicks
Consultant: Tony Buchanan

British Library Cataloguing in Publication Data

Gifford, Clive
    Cricket. – (Sporting skills)
    1. Cricket – Juvenile literature
    I. Title
    796.3'58

ISBN 9780750281195

Printed in China

10 9 8 7 6 5 4 3 2 1

Wayland is a division of Hachette Children's Books, an Hachette UK company.
www.hachette.co.uk

Picture credits
All photographs taken by Michael Wicks, except;
Cover Dreamstime.com/Eril Nisbett,
5 Philip Brown/Philip Brown/Corbis

Acknowledgements
The author and publisher would like to thank the following people for their help and participation in this book:
Old Albanian Cricket Club, Alison Finley, Terry James and Neil Dekker

The website addresses (URLs) included in this book were valid at the time of going to press. However, because of the nature of the Internet, it is possible that some addresses may have changed, or sites may have changed or closed down since publication. While the author and Publisher regret any inconvenience this may cause the readers, no responsibility for any such changes can be accepted by either the author or the Publisher.

Disclaimer
In preparation of this book, all due care has been exercised with regard to the advice, activities and techniques depicted. The publishers regret that they can accept no liability for any loss or injury sustained. When learning a new sport it is important to get expert tuition and to follow a manufacturer's instructions.

CONTENTS

WHAT IS CRICKET?

Cricket is an enthralling sport which calls on players to work hard together as a team. Teams take turns, known as innings, to bat and to score runs. The other team, the fielding side, tries to stop runs being scored and get the opposition batsmen out, known as taking a wicket. If one team loses ten wickets then its innings ends. The winning team is the one that scores the most runs in a match.

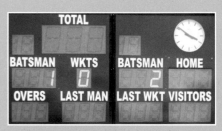

A cricket scoreboard shows the batting team's total score, the scores of the two batsmen who are in, the number of wickets taken, the number of overs bowled in this innings and the total score of the team when the last batsman was out along with his or her score.

OVERS AND ACTION

In the middle of the field is a narrow strip of ground called the pitch. A batsman stands at one end of the pitch and the bowler bowls the ball from the other end. A bowler bowls six times in a row from one end of the pitch. Each ball bowled is called a delivery and the six deliveries are called an over. However, if an umpire feels that a ball is too wide or high or that a delivery is a no ball (see page 25), then the bowler has to bowl that delivery again. At the end of an over, another bowler bowls from the opposite end of the pitch.

Scoring runs

1 This batsman hits the ball into space away from fielders. He has hit it to the right-hand side of the pitch, which for a right-handed batsman is known as the off side.

2 Watching the ball carefully, he judges that there is enough time to run to the other end of the pitch before the ball is thrown back. He calls to his partner to make a run.

3 The two batsmen cross as they run along the side of the pitch to swap ends. Batsmen must not run along the middle of the pitch or they will receive a warning from the umpire.

4 The batsman runs with his bat extended in front of him. The run is completed and added to his score only once he and the batsman at the other end have grounded their bats in the creases.

4

Away from playing a match, cricketers practise in cricket nets. These netted corridors allow a batsman to practise shots and a bowler to practise his or her bowling action.

CRICKET COMPETITIONS

Cricket is a hugely enjoyable game played by male and female teams of all ages and abilities. Most amateur games feature one innings per side and last a day or an evening with a maximum number of overs per side. At the elite level, top players are professionals, and play in competitions such as the English County Championship or the Australian Pura Cup. The very best cricketers get to play for their country against other top sides in Test matches. These can last up to five days with each side playing two innings.

While cricket balls used in many one-day games are white, a typical cricket ball is red and made of wool and cork covered in a leather case. This case is stitched together to form a raised seam around the middle of the ball.

England bowler Andrew Flintoff celebrates taking the wicket of an Australian batsman.

5

PITCH AND PLAYERS

A cricket team is made up of 11 players. All players may bat, some may bowl, while one player, the wicketkeeper, stands behind the stumps. The rest of the fielding team are directed into positions around the pitch by the captain of their side.

CRICKET KIT

In major one-day cricket competitions, adult players may wear coloured clothing. Usually, however, cricket is played in white clothing – white trousers and white shirts and sweaters. Batsmen and wicketkeepers wear lots of protective clothing. Some batsmen choose to wear a forearm guard on their front arms and also thigh pads underneath their trousers. All batsmen and wicketkeepers wear leg pads and male players tend to wear a protective box down their trousers.

handle

blade

Cricket bats vary in size and weight and smaller models are available for young players. Get your coach to advise you on a bat suitable for your age and size.

A fielder shows the basic cricket clothing worn by all players: white long trousers, shirt and shoes, which grip the ground. The fielder may also wear a white cricket jumper.

This batsman wears a protective helmet with a metal grille to protect his face from any deliveries that rear up sharply. He also wears padded batting gloves and leg pads.

This player is wearing leg pads and wicketkeeper gloves with webbing between the thumb and finger of the glove (see page 14). He is also wearing a sleeveless jumper.

The field and positions

The pitch is in the middle of the cricket field and at each end of the pitch are the wickets. Fielders are referred to by the position they are standing in. The positions here are shown for a right-handed batsman standing by the wicket at the top of the page. If the batsman were left-handed then the names of the fielding positions would be reversed. The field is also divided in half according to the batsman. If the batsman is right-handed, then the field on his right is called the off side and the field on his left is called the on, or leg side. These are reversed if the batsman is left-handed.

The edge of a cricket field is called the boundary. The boundary is usually marked by a rope. If a ball rolls or bounces over the rope, then four runs are awarded. If a ball clears the rope without bouncing, then six runs are awarded.

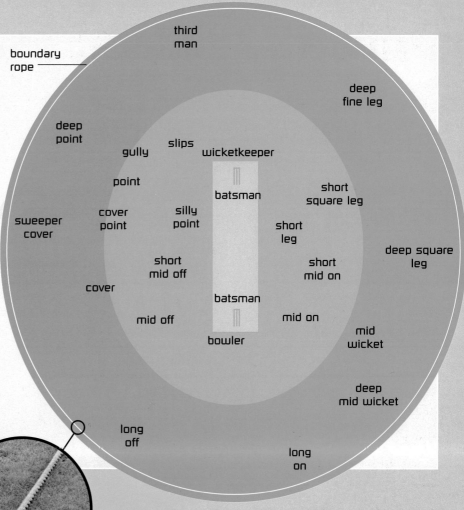

boundary rope

third man

deep fine leg

deep point

gully   slips   wicketkeeper

point

batsman

short square leg

cover point

silly point

short leg

sweeper cover

deep square leg

short mid off

short mid on

cover

batsman

mid off

bowler

mid on

deep mid wicket

mid wicket

long off

long on

CREASES AND WICKETS

The wickets consist of two small bails which sit on top of three stumps. These stumps are labelled according to whether the batsman is left- or right-handed. If the batsman is right-handed, then the stump on the right is called the leg stump, as this is on the leg side of the field, and the stump on the left is called the off stump, as this is on the off side of the field. These names swap if the batsman is left-handed. Surrounding the stumps are the creases. A batsman must ground his or her bat past the popping crease to not be run out. A bowler must ensure that part of his or her front foot is behind the popping crease, otherwise the delivery is a no ball (see page 25). On either side of these creases are two more lines, called return creases.

bails

off stump

leg stump

middle stump

popping crease

batting crease

UMPIRES AND LAWS

The laws of cricket are very complicated, but all young players must try to learn them. A match is run by umpires on the field who make rulings on events in the match. You should never argue with the umpires – their decisions are final.

In simple terms, a player can be out leg before wicket (lbw) if the ball hits the batsman's pads before the bat, and it would have gone on to hit the stumps, in the umpire's opinion. Here, the ball hits the batsman's pads in line with the stumps, so the umpire can give her out, lbw.

Here, the ball has hit the pads in line with the stumps but the batsman has stepped a long way forward. The umpire might decide that the ball would travel too high and miss the stumps and does not give her out.

If the ball's first bounce is on a line outside of leg stump, then the batsman cannot be out, lbw.

THE UMPIRES

While top international cricket has other officials, most amateur cricket matches are run by two umpires on the pitch. One usually stands behind the wicket at the same end as the bowler, while the other stands in line with the facing batsman but to the side at a position called square leg (see page 7). The umpires switch positions at the end of each over. The umpires are responsible for judging whether a run has been completed, whether a bowler has bowled a wide or no-ball, whether a batsman is in or out and all other matters on the field of play, including whether conditions are suitable for the game to continue.

The ball has pitched (bounced) wide of off stump but has moved in to hit the pads and may have hit the stumps. Because the batsman is not playing a shot, the umpire can give her out.

This batsman has been run out and will have to leave the field to be replaced by a team-mate. He has failed to get into his crease before the opposition fielder has broken the stumps with the ball.

To be in, a batsman has to have some part of his body or his bat behind the popping crease not just on the line.

The bat or some other part of the batsman's body must be grounded behind the line, and not just hovering above it.

IN OR OUT?

A batsman continues playing until the umpire signals that he or she is out with a raised finger. When the fielding players think a batsman may be out, they must appeal to the umpire and ask, 'How's that?' A batsman can be out in 11 different ways, but only six of these occur regularly. The first is bowled, when the ball hits the wicket and knocks off a bail. The second is caught, when a batsman's bat or the glove holding the bat connects with the ball and a fielder catches the ball before it touches the ground.

A third way a batsman can be out is if he or she knocks the bails off the stumps, in which case they are given out, 'hit wicket'. The fourth and fifth ways are leg before wicket (lbw – see page 8) and a run out (see above). The sixth is by stumping, when the facing batsman steps out of his or her popping crease, misses hitting the delivery and the wicketkeeper uses the ball to dislodge the bails before the batsman gets his or her bat back into the crease (see page 15).

Umpire signals

The umpire uses hand and body signals to communicate his or her decisions to the players and to the match scorer. Here is a collection of common umpiring signals.

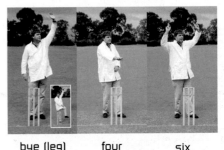

bye (leg)   four   six

no ball   wide   out

9

FIELDING

Many young cricketers see themselves as batsmen or bowlers, but all cricketers should consider themselves as fielders. Good fielding lifts the spirit of a team, frustrates opposition batsmen and can lead to stopping runs and even taking wickets through run-out chances.

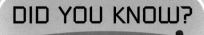
FIELDING PRACTICE

Many matches are won (and lost) by a small number of runs – runs that can be saved easily by good fielding. Fielding requires a lot of concentration, especially during a long match. Fielders must switch on as their bowler runs in and focus on the ball and where it is heading. If they have to field the ball, they should keep their eyes on the ball right into their hands. Stopping and retrieving the ball and returning it, usually to your wicketkeeper should be practised hard in training so that the techniques become second nature to you.

This fielder has got quickly into position behind the stumps to field a possible throw to the wicket. Another fielder stands behind her, backing up in case the throw is not on target or the first fielder fumbles.

1 For a ball running fast along the ground, the most secure method of stopping it is using the long barrier method. As the ball comes towards the fielder, he gets in line with its direction and drops to one knee, usually the opposite knee to his throwing hand.

Long barrier

2 His leg trails out to the side and his other foot is planted side-on to the ball with the heel touching the knee on the ground. He watches the ball into his hands.

3 As the ball arrives, the fielder gets his hands round both sides of the ball. The foot and leg form a barrier in case the ball bounces awkwardly.

1 This fielder is chasing the ball to stop it reaching the boundary. He sprints hard to cut off the ball. A successful chase and throw could see one, two or three runs prevented.

2 The fielder makes sure he reaches the ball with his throwing-arm side closest to the ball. He aims to pick up the ball close to his left foot.

3 The fielder stays low as he begins to put his weight on his right foot and pivots round so that his non-throwing shoulder faces forward.

4 As the player completes his turn, he brings his arm round to throw in the ball. The turning round and throwing action should all be one smooth movement.

Throwing from deep

1 With the ball in his throwing hand, the fielder drives up on his right leg. As he rises to an upright position, he takes his throwing arm back and turns his body to face side-on.

2 The fielder plants his left foot in line with the direction of his intended throw. His non-throwing arm also points ahead in the direction of the throw, which is usually to the wicketkeeper's end.

3 The fielder's throwing arm whips through as he transfers his body weight from his back foot to his front foot. As the throwing arm straightens, he releases the ball.

CATCHING

There are many sayings in cricket and one of the most important is 'catches win matches'. This is true at all levels of cricket. In Test match cricket, for example, batsmen are out more often due to catches than to being bowled or leg before wicket combined.

CATCHING PRINCIPLES

There are a number of different types of catch but certain principles apply to all of them. These include being decisive and calling for the catch to let team-mates know you are going for it. You must keep your eye on the ball and watch it like a hawk. Do not let crowd noise or any other distractions stop you from watching the ball right into your hands. Use a good catching technique (see right) and look to cushion the ball's impact with 'soft hands' as it arrives by bringing your hands back in the direction the ball was heading. Many catches are spilled at the last moment because the fielder has 'hard hands' from which the ball bounces out.

This girl is about to catch the ball using the overhand technique during catching practice. Catching improves only with repeated practice. Get your coach to arrange a varied range of catching and fielding drills to keep your training fresh.

Many catching chances come incredibly quickly to a fielder who may only be able to reach the ball with one hand. This fielder is diving to take a catch to his right-hand side. On landing, he must try to roll on his shoulder and back to keep the impact from jarring his elbow or hand which could cause the ball to fly out of his grip.

Here, three slip fielders form a line beside the wicketkeeper. They are positioned with their knees bent and feet more than shoulder-width apart. Their hands are cupped, waiting for a catch.

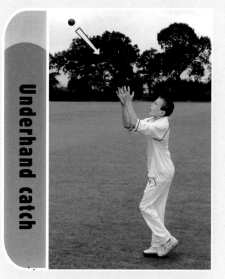

1 The fielder keeps his eyes on the ball with his hands high and his palms facing upwards.

2 Keeping his head still, he has cupped his hands together and spread his fingers.

3 The fielder gets his fingers around the ball and draws his hands into his body.

Overhand catch

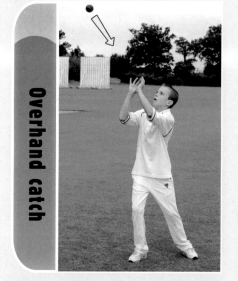

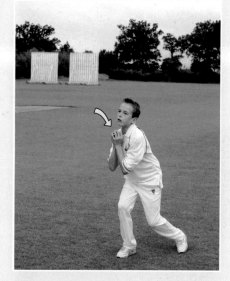

1 This fielder has raised his arms to catch the ball using the overhand or Australian method.

2 Watching the ball closely, the fielder's palms face the ball with the fingers spread wide and thumbs touching.

3 As the ball arrives, the fielder gets his hands around the ball and draws his hands back into his chest or just below one shoulder.

DROPPED!

If you drop a catch, do not get angry or act dazed. You must react immediately to field the ball and throw it back accurately to prevent runs. All players drop catches from time to time. Try to put it out of your mind and concentrate on staying alert for the next delivery and the next chance.

WICKETKEEPING

A fielding team in cricket is made up of bowlers, fielders and one wicketkeeper. The wicketkeeper has a vital role to play in taking wickets through catches, stumpings and run outs. He or she also stops runs and boosts the morale and chances of the team through tidy fielding and encouragement.

CLEAN KEEPING

The wicketkeeper's job is similar in some ways to a goalkeeper in football. He or she must be capable of concentrating for very long periods and repeatedly gathering the ball that has been bowled and passes a batsman. This must be done cleanly to avoid dropping a catching chance or to stop the ball running through so that the batsmen can take runs. Keepers need excellent fitness and flexibility to crouch behind the stumps for hours on end. A good wicketkeeping posture and technique, worked on with a coach, will help ease any strain.

This wicketkeeper has come up to the stumps to field closely behind them. As the ball is bowled, he rises slightly from his starting position keeping his knees bent and his chin up and eyes level watching the ball.

These wicketkeeping gloves have a pimpled surface on the palm and fingers for added grip and a webbed area between the first finger and the thumb to increase the catching area. Many gloves have a little padding for protection but must be flexible so that the wicketkeeper can get his or her hands around the ball.

Keepers have to be alert to a possible catch in front of the stumps. This wicketkeeper has left the stumps and is running to get under a high ball to try to take a catch.

POSITIONING

Wicketkeepers must judge how far back they should stand behind the stumps and this will vary with each bowler. It may be a number of paces to a fast bowler or between half and one full pace to a slow bowler. Many keepers choose to stand fractionally towards the off stump side so that they can watch the flight of the ball and because they expect the ball to come to them on an off stump line. All wicketkeepers, though, have to be prepared for surprising deliveries that veer down the leg side, keep very low or rear up sharply.

As runs are taken by the batsmen, this wicketkeeper has moved up to the stumps. He is calling for the ball to be thrown to him.

Taking the ball

1 This keeper is about to take a ball travelling down the off side. He has stepped across with his right foot to get into line with the ball's flight.

2 The wicketkeeper gathers the ball with his arms relaxed. He cushions its arrival by bending his elbows to move the hands back on impact.

3 Leg-side deliveries can be tricky to spot because they are hidden by the batsman. This wicketkeeper has stepped across to the leg side so that he can catch with both hands.

Stumping

1 This batsman has stepped out of his crease to play a shot and has missed the ball. The wicketkeeper has already risen and is in line with the ball's flight.

2 The wicketkeeper gathers the ball safely. Leaning in so that his bodyweight is over the foot nearest the stumps, he sweeps his hands down towards the stumps.

3 The wicketkeeper dislodges the bails and appeals to the umpire. The batsmen's rear foot is out of the crease, so the umpire should give the batsman out.

BATTING BASICS

Between five and seven players in a side are usually selected for their skills as a batsman, but all the players in a team may be asked to bat. The last few batsmen in a side are called the tailenders, and their runs can often be the difference between winning or losing a match.

STANCE

When standing in front of the wicket, you should adopt the basic batting stance where you are side on with your front shoulder pointing down the pitch. Although your knees need to be flexed and the bat facing the direction the ball comes from, try to stand tall and not crouch. Some players find resting the bat on the top of their back foot helps this. From this ready stance, a batsman should be nicely balanced and able to move so that he or she can play forward or back to a delivery.

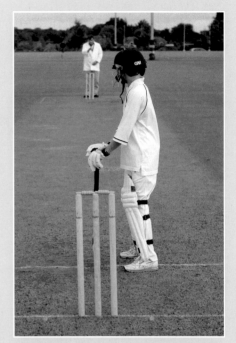

This batsman has just come in and is taking guard. This means that he asks the umpire to help him line up his bat with middle stump or between the middle and leg stumps. He may make a small scratch on the pitch to remind him of this position.

This batsman is in a good, balanced stance ready to face the bowling. Her front shoulder points down the pitch and her weight is balanced between both feet. These are around shoulder-width apart and either side of the popping crease. Her head is turned and is as level as possible and facing the bowling.

From the ready position, the batsman takes her bat back. This is the backlift. Keeping focused on the bowler's arm, she aims for a smooth backlift taking the bat back over the stumps and cocking her wrists so that the bat face points to the slips. Depending on the shot she plays, she will either step forward or back.

2 The batsman bends his front knee to get his body weight forward and extends his back leg with this foot on the ground. He brings his bat forward keeping it parallel with his leg pad and angles the bat handle forward ahead of the bat blade to keep the ball down as he connects.

1 This batsman looks to play a forward defensive, the most basic stroke. He starts to bring his bat down and lets his front shoulder lead into the stroke. His top hand controls the bat with the bottom hand gripping gently.

Close-up, you can see how the bat is angled forwards and forms a barrier to the ball with the front pad. Playing the ball with 'soft hands', allowing the bat to give a little, cushions the ball's impact.

Grip

The bat is gripped with both hands wrapping around the handle. The top hand grips the bat handle relatively tightly. If you are right-handed, then the top hand is your left hand. The back of the top hand faces down the pitch. The bottom hand has a looser grip and is placed below the top hand with both hands meeting in the middle of the handle.

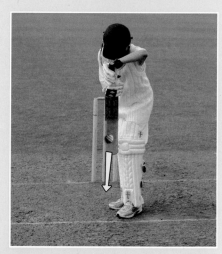

1 This batsman is facing a ball that is bouncing about waist high. As the ball bounces, the batsman will step back and across towards off stump to get in line with the ball.

2 With his weight mainly on his back foot, the batsman brings the bat down keeping his front elbow high. The shot is played with no follow-through so that the ball drops straight to the ground.

PLAYING SHOTS

To become good batsmen, players need a range of different strokes they can play to deliveries coming towards them at different speeds, heights, lines and angles. The length of a delivery is very important, as a batsman decides whether to play on his or her front foot or step back and play a back-foot shot.

DIFFERENT PITCHES AND LENGTHS

Cricket pitches can vary in the amount of pace they have and how much hardness or bounce they generate. A dry, rock-hard pitch, for example, will tend to see the ball bounce higher. A batsman has to judge the pace and bounce of the pitch so that they can choose the right shot to play. They also have to judge the length of a delivery – where the ball first lands (pitches) on the pitch, as this will greatly influence their choice of shot.

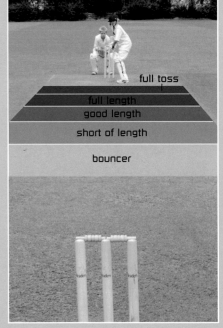

This image shows the various lengths of deliveries. Shorter pitched deliveries, such as a bouncer tend to rise higher, while, at the other end of the scale, a full toss does not bounce before it reaches the batsman. A good length ball is one that puts the batsman in two minds as to whether to play forward or back.

Front foot off drive

1 This left-handed batsman goes to play a front-foot shot called the off drive. This is usually played to a full-length delivery or a half volley bouncing around or just outside off stump.

2 The batsman steps onto his front foot. The bat swings forwards and needs to be timed so that the ball is hit with the batsman's head directly over it.

3 The hands lead the bat in its follow through with the rear shoulder (the shoulder of the bottom hand) passing under the batsman's chin. The follow through sees the bottom arm straighten.

18

1 The movement back to perform a backwards defensive can be harnessed to play a driving or forcing shot off the back foot. This shot is played to a shorter ball which has not risen above stump height.

2 The batsman starts to step back into his crease and begins to bring his bat down more quickly than with the backward defensive shot. This will help to generate extra power.

3 He has to time the movement of his bottom hand, which drives the bat to punch through the ball. This must not happen too early otherwise the ball will be sent up into the air.

4 The batsman completes the shot by following through. The bat should be pointing in the direction that the ball is heading.

A cut shot can be played to a ball that has pitched short and wide of the off stump. The batsman moves his back foot across his stumps and brings the bat round so that it is horizontal. The wrists should roll over, angling the bat face down as the bat connects with the ball and follows through.

19

MORE SHOTS

The three shots shown on the previous pages were all strokes that send the ball to the off side. Here are three further strokes which, if hit correctly, see the ball travel to the leg side.

LEG-SIDE SHOTS

Most bowlers aim for the ball to pitch on or just outside off stump. As a result, more of the fielders are stationed on the off side than the leg side. Common fielding arrangements have only two or three fielders on the on or leg side of the cricket field. Leg-side shots tend to be trickier for beginners to master but are vital. A batsman with good leg-side shots can use deliveries that stray down the leg side and hit them into large unguarded areas of the pitch to score runs.

The back-foot leg glance is a relatively common shot played to both fast and slow bowling where the ball has pitched just outside leg stump. In contrast, the sweep is played only against slow bowlers and the hook is played only against fast bowlers who have attempted a bouncer.

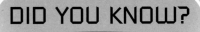

Leg glance

1 The back-foot leg glance is all about timing. The batsman steps back, making sure that his pads still protect his leg stump.

2 The batsman starts to turn his body and moves his front foot so that his stance changes from a side-on to a chest-on posture.

3 The batsman then brings the bat round. The shot is to be played with the bat close to the body and the batsman must wait for the ball to come onto his bat.

4 At the last moment, the batsman's wrists turn and the bottom hand helps turn the bat face round to deflect the ball down the leg side.

1 This batsman plays a sweep shot to a ball bouncing outside leg stump. He moves his front foot forwards, close to the bounce or pitch of the ball.

2 The front leg is bent at the knee and the back leg bends low. The bat is swung round in a wide path in front of the player.

3 The bat is close to horizontal as it travels in front of the batsman. His wrists start to roll over to angle the bat face down.

4 The wrists continue rolling as the arms swing on to the follow through. The shot does not to have to be hit with great power but with good timing to send the ball down the leg side.

1 This batsman looks to play a hook shot at a ball that is rising to chest height. He moves his front leg back and towards the leg side to give himself room.

2 The batsman swings the bat round with his hands high and arms parallel to the ground. He leans away from the ball to play the shot with his arms straight.

3 He connects with the full face of the bat. As he connects, he rolls his wrists so that the ball does not travel too high in the air.

21

BATTING TACTICS

It takes more than a range of good strokes to score a large innings in cricket. Batsmen need many other attributes including patience, concentration and the ability to change the pace of an innings depending on the conditions.

PATIENCE AND PACING

Patience is vital for a batsman – one rash stroke can lead to your wicket falling. Top batsmen try to decide what shot to play based on each delivery. This means defending a good, testing delivery from a bowler but looking to attack a poor ball that may be wide or short.

SHOT SELECTION

Making the right shot decision comes only with experience and plenty of practice in the nets. Your choice of shot often depends on the speed, line and length of the delivery. It may also depend on where the fielders are placed. Batsmen keep an eye on changes to the positions of fielders and aim to play the ball away from danger and into gaps to score runs.

Nudge and run

This batsman has spotted that the field is placed deep (near the boundary) on the off side to stop strong shots. He moves to play a forward defensive shot but angles his bat a little to nudge the ball gently into the off side. With the ball travelling slowly and into space, there is time for him to set off for a quick run. His batting partner should have spotted the opportunity and already be advancing down the pitch.

Rising ball

1 A good batsman is able to judge when to play and when to leave a ball. This batsman is facing a fast bowler and is aware that the ball may be pitched short to rise up sharply.

2 The batsman has spotted that the delivery is a bouncer aimed straight at him. Deciding to leave the ball, he leans back, keeps his bat down, and follows the ball with his eyes.

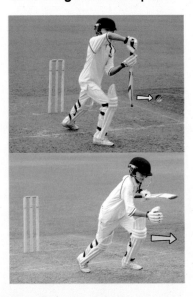

1 Sometimes, batsmen may need to be really aggressive. This batsman is facing a slow bowler and is on the attack.

2 He spots a delivery that is bouncing short and moves his feet quickly to get close to the pitch of the ball to play an attacking stroke.

3 With no one on the boundary behind the bowler, he looks to play a lofted drive. This is similar to a straight drive but with the ball sent a lot higher.

4 The batsman avoids leaning back as he plays the shot. He swings the bat through strongly. The bat connects with the ball just after the ball has bounced.

Lofted drive

5 The batsman ends the stroke with a high follow through. The ball travels straight, usually dropping in the field and may reach the boundary for four runs.

This young batsman raises his bat to celebrate scoring a half-century (50 runs). To score a half-century or century (100 runs) is a great achievement, but the batsman must get back to concentrating hard to continue building his team's score.

BUILDING PARTNERSHIPS

As an innings progresses, pairs of batsmen try to form long and profitable partnerships with each encouraging the other between overs. Batsmen need good communication between each other as they form a batting partnership. This is especially the case when running between the wickets. Good calling by the two players can enable them to score quick single runs that can keep the score ticking along. Poor communication leads to many lost wickets due to run outs.

BOWLING BASICS

Bowlers deliver the ball in many different ways. They can vary the speed at which they bowl – usually split into fast, medium and slow – and whether they try to spin the ball, make it swing through the air or make the ball land on its seam and move off the pitch.

THE BOWLING ACTION

A bowler's movements to deliver the ball are called the bowling action. This starts with the run-up to the wicket, which is carefully marked out and may be a couple of paces for a slow bowler or 20 or more paces for a fast bowler. The bowler's run-up ends with the delivery stride, when the bowling arm swings round and the ball is released. Bowlers can choose to bowl either 'over the wicket', when the wicket is on the same side as their bowling arm, or 'around the wicket', when the wicket is on the other side to their bowling arm.

DID YOU KNOW?

With 502 wickets, Wasim Akram of Pakistan has taken more one-day international wickets than any other player.

This bowler has measured out her run-up and is placing a marker on the ground. This shows where she needs to start her run-up for each delivery.

The basic grip for seam bowling sees the first and middle fingers grip either side of the seam with the thumb on the bottom. The ball should be resting on the last joints of the fingers.

1 This left-handed, medium-pace bowler is in his run-up to the stumps. He aims to keep his running smooth and rhythmical.

2 The bowler takes his delivery stride with his right foot. His right arm is held high and he looks over his right shoulder straight down the pitch at the far stumps.

3 The bowler plants his right foot pointing down the pitch and is fully side-on as his bowling arm comes over.

The two most common causes of an umpire signalling a no ball are shown here. The first shows how no part of the bowler's front foot is behind the popping crease – being on the line is not enough. The second shows the bowler's back foot outside the return crease. It must be completely inside the return crease for the delivery to be a legal one.

popping crease

return crease

4 After release, the bowling arm continues to follow through. The arm moves past his body as the left foot starts to take the next step.

5 The bowler lands with his left foot straight down the pitch. He keeps his eye on the far end of the pitch in case the ball comes back his way.

NO BALLS

An umpire will signal a no-ball for a range of reasons. The two most common are due to a bowler's footwork (see left) but there are other reasons. These include if the bowler does not tell the umpire which side of the wicket he or she is bowling from. Full tosses which reach the batsman above waist height without bouncing are often called as a no ball. When a no ball is called, one run is added to the batting team's score and the delivery has to be bowled again. If the batsman hits the no ball, he or she cannot be out bowled, lbw, caught, stumped or hit wicket, but can however, still be run out.

SEAM AND SWING

Fast- and medium-pace bowlers must be able to bowl with accuracy time and time again. They may also vary the speed or placement of their deliveries to get a wicket. Bowlers can get the ball to change direction suddenly by bouncing it off the ball's seam. This is called seam bowling. They can also make it swerve in the air. This is called swing bowling.

ACCURACY AND REPETITION

Building accuracy in your bowling action so that you can place the ball repeatedly in the same area time after time can gain many wickets by itself. An over full of good deliveries with no wide balls can put pressure on batsmen, sometimes forcing them into a rash shot, which leads to a wicket.

Some pitches help seam bowlers with sideways movement off the seam as the ball bounces or different, unpredictable levels of high and low bounce. On such a pitch, an experienced seam bowler will concentrate on bowling accurately and letting the pitch do the work to make the ball deceive the batsman.

The sightscreens are placed off the field of play behind the bowler so that the batsman gets a clear sight of the bowler's arm during a delivery. Sightscreens are usually on wheels so that they can be moved depending on the bowler's angle.

This is an attacking field set for a bowler getting movement off the seam or swinging the ball away in the air. The three slip fielders are in position for a catch off the edge of the bat, while the gully fielder (left) needs quick reactions to stop runs and take potential catches from shots that the batsman hits in the air.

gulley

slips

wicketkeeper

SWING BOWLING

Some medium-pace and faster bowlers are able to swerve or swing the ball in the air. This can make life very hard for the batsman, but it is a tricky skill to master. Swing depends on the weather conditions and keeping one side of the ball polished and shiny and the other side rough. When a bowler is able to swing the ball, he or she tends to pitch the ball closer to the batsman as this gives the ball more time to swing through the air.

To swing the ball into a right-handed batsman, the ball is gripped so that the polished, shiny side of the ball is on the left. This delivery is called an inswinger. A good inswinger can deceive a batsman and get between the bat and pad to hit the stumps.

To swing the ball away from a right-handed batsman, the ball is gripped so that the shiny side of the ball is on the right side. This is called an away or outswinger and it can lead to a catch by the wicketkeeper or a slip fielder.

VARYING LINES AND LENGTHS

Once you are happy with your bowling action, you and your coach can start exploring how you can add variation to your deliveries. Sometimes, this is as simple as just changing your line a little. For instance, if a batsmen keeps on stepping in front of the stumps, you may want to aim a delivery straight at the wicket, looking for an lbw. Changes in the speed of deliveries can also surprise batsmen. For example, a slower ball may see the batsman play a shot too early and give a catching chance.

SPIN BOWLING

Spin bowling is slower than swing or seam bowling. The bowler's grip and bowling action make the ball spin quickly so that it may move dramatically in one direction or another when it lands on the pitch. There are two main types of spin bowling; off-spin and leg-spin.

OFF-SPIN BOWLING

An off-spin bowler uses his fingers to put lots of spin on the ball so that the ball bounces on the off side and then moves towards the leg side of a right-handed batsman. An off-spinner will vary the pace of his or her deliveries a little and may sometimes send a ball in a higher loop through the air or bowl a quicker, flatter delivery towards the batsman. These changes of flight can deceive and confuse a batsman. Many off-spinners also learn to use an 'arm ball'. This is a delivery that has little or no spin so that it travels straight on instead of turning towards the leg stump when it bounces.

Spin bowling

1 This right-handed off-spinner has completed the few paces of his run-up and is entering his delivery stride.

2 As he plants his left foot, he keeps his non-bowling arm high and is focused on where he wants to pitch the ball.

3 He brings his bowling arm over, while keeping his head still.

4 As the bowling arm comes over, he twists his body vigorously, flicks his fingers to give the amount of spin he wants, and follows through.

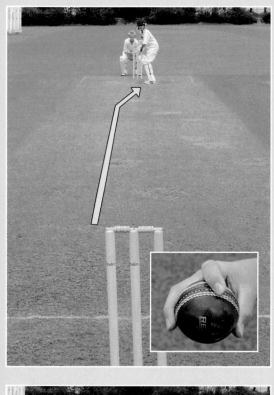

For an off-spin delivery, the ball is held in the fingers. The spin is created by twisting the first and middle fingers and wrist sharply in a clockwise direction.

LEG-SPIN BOWLING

Leg-spin bowling sees the ball turn from the leg side to the off side. It involves a strong wrist action to generate a rapidly spinning ball. Top leg-spinners have some other tricky deliveries, including a top spinner that tends to travel straight on after it bounces. One of the most important variations is the 'googly'. This is a ball released out of the back of the hand that spins the opposite way to a normal leg-spinner – a good googly may turn towards leg side and catch the edge of a batsman's bat offering a close catch.

For a normal leg-spin delivery, the ball is gripped by the top of the index and middle fingers, which lie across the seam of the ball. The ball is released with a powerful flick of the wrist with the third finger dragging along the seam, spinning the ball anti-clockwise.

SPIN BOWLING SKILLS

Apart from accuracy and the ability to spin the ball, a spin bowler needs other skills to be successful. He or she needs to master variations in their spin bowling to trick the batsman, and patience to bowl for long periods to put the batsman under pressure. They also need a strong, positive attitude as a batsman may attack their bowling and score a lot of runs.

slip

wicketkeeper

short leg

silly point

This batsman is about to face a delivery from an off-spinner. An attacking field has been set and this includes a slip and a silly point who are positioned to catch the ball if it comes off the bat and pad and pops up into the air.

GLOSSARY AND RESOURCES

Glossary

around the wicket When a bowler bowls with the wicket on the other side of the body to his or her bowling arm.

backing up A fielder who gets behind a team-mate who is standing by the stumps to stop the ball if a throw is inaccurate or fumbled.

bails The two wooden cylinders placed on top of the three stumps to form a wicket.

bouncer A commonly-used term for a fast, short-pitched ball that bounces high.

century Usually used to mean when an individual batsman has scored 100 runs. A score of 50 runs is known as a half-century.

flight The path of the ball through the air.

full toss A delivery that reaches the batsman from the bowler's hand without hitting the pitch first.

lbw The usual abbreviation for leg before wicket, a way of a batsman being out when the ball hits the batsman's pads when they are in front of the wicket.

leg side The side of a cricket field on the left for a right-handed batsman and on the right for a left-handed batsman.

leg-spin bowling When a delivery bounces from a batsman's leg side towards his or her off stump.

length This is a term used to describe how far up the cricket pitch a delivery bounces after it has left the bowler's hand.

off side The side of a cricket field on the right for a right-handed batsman and on the left for a left-handed batsman.

off-spin bowling When a delivery bounces from a batsman's off side towards his or her leg stump.

over the wicket When a bowler bowls with the wicket on the same side of the body to his or her bowling arm.

partnership The runs scored by a pair of batsmen batting together.

seam bowling When a bowler makes the ball bounce off the seam at different angles.

spin bowling When a bowler spins the ball so that it bounces away at different angles.

swing bowling When a bowler is able to make the ball swerve or swing in the air.

umpires The people who judge whether or not a wicket has fallen and other decisions regarding the laws of cricket. Usually there are two umpires, but in professional cricket matches there may be a third umpire who examines video replays when the other umpires cannot reach a decision.

wide A delivery which, in the umpire's opinion, is too wide of a batsman to reach. In most competitions, a run is added to the batting team's score and the ball is bowled again.

Diet and nutrition

Cricket once had a reputation of being a sport of skill but not fitness. That has all changed. Far more emphasis is now put on fast and athletic fielding while the fitter and better prepared a player is, the more likely he or she will be able to concentrate well as they bat for long periods or bowl at peak performance for many overs.

Cricketers need to warm up in advance of their match using routines developed by their coach who can also advise young players on a good, healthy diet. Eating a balanced meal several hours or more before a match gives your body time to digest it. Try to avoid fast foods with high levels of fat and sugar and concentrate on healthy eating of foods such as fresh fruit and vegetables, lean meats, chicken, fish, rice and pasta. During a major break in a game, look to eat a light, healthy meal or snack such as muesli bars or fruit. Make sure you drink plenty of water to replace fluids lost during a long match.

www.harrowdrive.com/the-complete-guide-to-cricket-nutrition/
A collection of articles on diet and nutrition for cricketers.

www.mypyramid.gov/kids/index.html
Balanced, healthy eating can be shown as a food pyramid. This website contains lots of downloadable fact files on the food pyramid and nutrition.

Resources

www.icc-cricket.com
The website of the International Cricket Council (ICC), the organisation that runs world cricket.

news.bbc.co.uk/sport1/hi/cricket/skills/default.stm
The BBC's cricket webpages includes handy information on the laws of cricket and video masterclasses of top players performing bowling, batting and fielding techniques.

www.rlca.com.pk/tips.asp
A collection of tips, many with photographs from the Rashid Latif Coaching Academy.

www.cricketweb.net/coaching/index.php
An excellent instructional website with lots of coaching drills and ideas and tips for improving your batting, bowling and fielding.

www.webbsoc.demon.co.uk
A website devoted to women's cricket with lots of news about players, matches and competitions and links to other sites.

www.cricinfo.com
For facts and stats fans, this is the ultimate website with records, news and details of every Test match and one-day international and lots of other features.

www.fitness4cricket.com
A website devoted to improving and maintaining peak fitness to play cricket with drills and advice about recovering from injuries.

INDEX